POWER OF TEENS PEN

THIS IS A POETRY BOOK. IN THIS BOOK YOU CAN FIND A LOT OF INTERESTING POEMS RELATED TO LOVE LIFE ETC.

STUTI GUPTA

DEDICATED TO MY PARENTS AND MY MOTHERLAND

INDIA, AND ALSO I WOULD THANK MY TEACHERS FOR
SUPPORT

FOR MAKING MY JOURNEY POSSIBLE

ON THE BOOK

POWER OF TEENS PEN

Contents

Foreword

"power of a teens pen"

In this poetry book the reader can find fascinating poems. The author of this poetry book is Stuti Gupta. Stuti is a small town girl who loves to read and write. She chose the title of book as " POWER OF A TEENS PEN" because she believes that whatever she thought, it was incomplete without her pen she think that there is a lot of power in a teens pen.

This book has poems related to love, sadness, happiness and more.

The team thanks you that you bought this book and took out your precious time to read this.

Acknowledgements

ACKNOWLEDGMENTS

To all my readers, to whom I want to share all the sets of my poems which are based on many fascinating events of my life. I am going to write a book so soon, so stay tuned and keep supporting after publishing this book, all this belongs to you. I hope I will fulfill all your hopes with this when you realize that all the poems in this book have something connective with the readers and a long story behind them. I have chosen this platform to share something with you, not to gain fame. Your love for reading my book is all I want.

TO Shubra Saxena , an amazingly teacher who was there with me always behind me when I was developing the core concepts of this book. From starting to the arrival, and supported me in every possible manner.

To Mihika Kumari who have been my great friend and have been with me all the time and also supported me.

To Piyush Baindara who have been such a great inspiratin to me. He is also the writer of RANIKHET EXPRESS-THE LOVE TRACK. Thank you for your guidance and support.

To my parents who made me what I am today and inspired me for all this.

To Nikhil Gupta my father who have supported me till end.

To Meenal singh who have been the best one to support me and she the first reader and first one to comment on this book

1. valley of uttarakhand

{ uttarakhand it is a beautiful land, also known as land of god and goddess, the author of this book belongs from a small town in uttarakhand this is the first poem of this book based on the life of uttarakhand, the poem is titled as VALLEY OF UTTARAKHAND}

1. Valley of uttarakhand

Green grass, wind blows.
High mountains, curvy roads
Pleasant weather sometimes it rains,
Sometimes its sunny with the dried drain
From here the Himalaya is clear
In the morning it is like the silver stair.
The sun rays hit the snow,
Giving a beautiful view and making us blow
Organic farming, organic people
With a charming smile
Just like any nature sweetener.
The Char Dham is alluring pilgrimage,
The tigers of Corbett have their own privilege.
Travel here whenever you get time,
To keep dizziness away take some lime.
The beauty of the nature given by god
Admiring the mountains.
Land of devtas. It seem to be

It is created differently, amazingly

It is our uttarakhand…!

2. self love best love

{keep taking time for yourself until you are you again. Love yourself unconditionally, just as you love those closest to you despite their fault. Love yourself first and everything else falls into line, the author of this book wrote a beautiful poem on self love.}

2. Self-love best love

Once when I was running,

From all that haunted me ;

To the dark I was succumbing

To what hurt unbearably.

Searching for the one thing,

That would set my sad soul free.

In time I stumbled upon it,

An inner calm and peace;

And now I am beginning,

To see and to believe,

In who I am becoming-

And all I have yet to be.

3. a thousand versions of you

{ you all may see yourself in many different forms sometimes when you are happy you have a different version of you sometimes when you excited and sad at the same time a new version of you appear, just to define the thousand versions of yourself stuti wrote a short poem titles "A THOUSAND VERSIONS OF YOU" }

3. A THOUSAND VERSIONS OF YOU
You have shed
A thousand skins
To become the person
You are today!
And if you ever feel
Overwhelmed
By the many people
You once were,
Remember,
Your bones have grown,
But what makes them
Has never changed.

4. learning to let you go

{we all have that one person in our life who we love more than us but what if that person does not care we feel hurt inside of loosing it but sometimes it's good we loose them or go far away for their life here's poem number 4 titled " LEARNING TO LET YOU GO" }

4. LEARNING TO LET YOU GO!

Waiting for the moment I can let you go,

Never been so calm in life,

It's a stillness even I am scared of,

There was this moment that hold me captive,

And I am still in that moment

Distance never made sense to me,

I wonder what's it going to take,

Now-a-days I get lost in the moment

What is this feeling curving into my hearts,

My mind is lost, and these

Feeling breaking me down,

And I can't let you go

I hold on to the dream

Even it's heavy on my mind,

I will never cause any trouble,

I am learning to let you go…..!

5. a friend called sucess

{ every one has a friend, but eveyone's best friend is success. To be best friends with success you need to do hardwork , the author has wrote a poem called A FRIEND CALLED SUCCESS let's have a sneek peek into her poem}

5.A Friend Called SUCCESS…!

Success is a friend to

Those who persevere

He is free and very fair

He speaks but they don't hear

So failure puts them to fear

They can't find success

But he lives near

The street of determination

Seek him in your imagination

And you will find him in your vision

You can't achieve success in force

But perseverance and endurance

For he keep changing his location

Through innovation….!

6. why me?

{ in our life this situation must have came In which we reply why me?. Even the author herself confessed that her sentences used to be incomplete without the words why me? During her exams time stuti wrote this poem titled why me? Let's see what all she wrote during exams }

6.WHY ME?
If you have to ask WHY ME?
When you are feeling really blue
When the world has turned against you
And you don't know what to do
When it pours colossal raindrops
And the road's winding mess
And you are feeling more confused
Than you ever could express,
When the saddened sun won't shine
When the stars will not align,
When you'd rather be
Inside your bed,
The covers pulled
And your head
When life is something
That you dread
And you have to ask WHY ME?......
Then when the world seems right and true,
When rain has left a gentle dew

When you feel happy being YOU
Plese ask yourself WHY ME? The too....!

7. why god made teachers

{ TEACHER we call all those people with this name who teach us something the author said that she will always have a soft corner in her heart for some special teachers though she (the author) is in class 8th but there were two teachers who were too close to her heart. The first one is her class teacher Meenal ma'am and the second her sister who always taught her that what's right and what's wrong. She wrote a sweets poem dedicated to all her teachers and ofcourse those two special one titled WHY GOD MADE TEACHERS?}

7.WHY GOD MADE TEACHERS?

When god created teachers

He gave us special friends

To help us understand his world

And truly comprehend

The beauty and the wonder

Of everything we see

And became a better person

With each discovery

When god created teachers

He gave us special guides

To show us way in which to grow

So we can all decide

How to live and how to do

What's right instead of wrong

To lead us so that we can lead

And learn how to be strong

Why god created teachers
In his wisdom and his grace
Was to help us learn and make our world
A better wiser place…!

8. ceasing bolishie

{ here comes the poem number 8 but it's fascinating as the author herself can't tell that on what topic it is she randomly wrote this poem so let's have a look on the poem titled CEASING BOLISHIE}

8.CEASING BOLISHIE

You are stubborn, me a lover

You are candle, with blazing wick

Me a moth in the love sick

I'm blazed ye blaze 'tis a fame

Ye are proud of thy splendor

Me finds my love everything

It is the slave it is the king

Trial me, trial thee do claim

Let's see who wins the game

Ye scare of unrolling disgrace

Me shock of thy severance

Ye lack means of love thence

My nerves are out of frame

Let's see who wins the game

If my leaving soul leaves it's place

D live in the vale of thy heart

And no more it would be apart

To you then the love 'l claim

Let's see who wins the game

When the shade of thy bolshie

Would lose it's long long length

And cease mighty raging strength
Say then the winning game
And see who wins the game.

9. the edge of night

9. The edge of the night
A table spread in a tomb, dinner for the dead
the dead! Why did you pay a visit to my eyes last night?

Night is the time for angels of dreams
we who, each of us, will one day return
to our hungry mother the grave. The darkness comes
from knowing nothing is ours, except death

takes bites out of my heart. O Asclepius pupil
teacher Chiron, please bring medicine
to my dead love, and I forever understudy
will attempt some sort of attainment

to wake with a sore splitting back from the cold floor
in borrowed clothes and eyes, lent by a saint
giving at the same time an encompassing embrace
'Friend, ' is all he said in tears, heart big enough to feed

this dead world. To wake up and see the sun
if not the glare from beyond, glittering
on broken glass, beside stretched roadside
where some had sprayed symbolic worlds and signs

scars full of flowers – to wake is to see
again this unusual world, whose secret cannot be known
until we enter the sky, or the earth
takes the edge off the night, the memory of your smile
Judging this town of sleep, I found it had already been judged
the Lord on his axe-cut cross of cypress
he is an incurable domestic bore
a family man, who never swore a word

an only child with a hollow mother
full with the carved cares of a household
wearing his poverty as a coat of arms
for eyes to look upon that beheld no bravura of vision.
The crisp grass rattles and shakes ripely, dryly
and all of this in fidelity to death
it was the same old same old, the hard husk of the ego
won't ever resolve, yet grinds down hard internally

into the swirl, the wine bitter-soaked seed
labouring lie - vice is kindled, burned in loins that melt
peculiar smiles alive, of all hope
has gone to explore the forlorn desert all alone

far away from the security of grim towns

where a girl is safe searching numbly in the comfort of fear.
You have gone or strayed away, never to be found
I sit and hear sour hiss of traffic calling

this burned and gutted ghost, vague semblance of time
on and off like one long sick light-switch
electric dream/confused state of everyone
greedy for dead love, drain her life, her soul

from every side for me. Greatest dribbling cannibal
tired Bolshie future, sleep . . . with disease.

III

Torn in two, I stand between, the idol and the grave
I do not know anything, I do not know. I do not
of this world, know anything – nor do I want to
but I have misled the past and will do so again

bring the teachers to the fore, let them stand
and be accounted as emperors of their own disease
and demise. As the sky claps the earth - wrings blood
from all rocks and far away I fly, every day

from the storm in the brain. The science of the mind
corroded the body, blinded every mile I ever burnt
in this life and the next if there ever were such a thing

10. my confession

{ so here is the poem number 10 all about love confession, have you ever confessed to a person about how you feel about him/her well if not then you are just like stuti, stuti said then when she was in secondary school she had a crush and she had crush on him for about 3 years wow that a long time period but she always felt nervous to let him know that she had a crush on him. After a point of time she realized that having a crush is not bad but not letting them know is she realized that we never know that when our life will end so we must confess our feeling to the person who we love so she wrote this poem titled MY CONFESSION }

10. MY CONFESSION

My love for you is uncontrollable

My feelings for you are unstoppable

Can't go a day without thinking about you

Without you I am not complete

With you my heart finds a beat

My heart is filled with joy because of your love

You are my strength and without you I'm weak

Before you came into my life I was

Hopeless, lonely, sad

When you showed up I knew you were sent to me

You are always here to cheer me up.

Your smile makes me shy

And sometimes I wonder where you have been all this while

But I am just glad that I managed to get you in my life

11. they say

{ the society, if we talk about the society so we all know that every person have a different mindset and due to this THEY SAY a lot of things. Some are even helpful but some even make no sense. Stuti lived in a very different environment in which she had to give importance to society's decision more than her own that was the time when stuti took a step for herself and decided to make a career}

11. THEY SAY

They say I'm sorry for your loss
They say your heart will mend
They say you're in a better place
And death is not the end.
They say you're reunited
With loved ones gone before
They say that you'll be waiting
When I walk through heavens door
I feel their love in each word
And comfort they impart
And known that each is spoken
From deep within the heart
But all the words of comfort
Though kind, sincere and true
Can't take away the emptiness
I'm feeling without you

12. don't ask if i'm okay

12. DON'T ASK IF I'M OKAY
Don't ask me how I'm doing
Don't ask if I'm okay
Don't say they're in a better place
As you won't like what I say
No...... time is not a healer
And this was not gods will
If he knew how much I've really lost
They would be right here still
I won't try to be positive
And this wasn't for the best
My heart's in broken pieces
And it hurts deep in my chest
Don't say at least they're out of pain
Well I'm not, and may never be
Their pain is gone, but mine's still here
it's been passed on to me
Don't tell me, you know how I feel
Even though it may be true!
This grief is mine
For what length of time.....
It takes me to get through

13. lonely old soul

13. LONELY OLD- SOUL
I had always dreamt
Of having a loving caring family
To cherish and to embrace, forever and a day
But how time drifts by quietly,
Unnoticed and divorce does
Take it's toll
I have now lived alone for night on 30 years
And watched unwaittingly
As time blended slothfully into oneness
Seconds, and even minutes tickling
Seamlessly into the emptiness,
That is the darkened soul
Searching night
I hear the incessant
Screaming echoing,
Through, and through my mind
As all becomes one continuous, flowing
Stream within, one's tired
Soulful and fragile spirited head.
There is , but one saving grace you know
For those that do not seek the sanctuary
Of the place within
Though very small, it is; as the night
Becomes the day, and day becomes the

Night
With dreams becoming one's reality and the
Daytime.
Night marish meanderings
While always trying to count one's
Blessing
The good, the bad and indifferent
I can't for the life of me, help me,
From gazing, many endless
Fruitless hours
Out of my window to see if, long
Forgotten family , friends or
Even foes are coming to visit this
Poor, old-lonely soul....

14. a prodigal

14. A PRODIGAL

The brown enormous odor he lived by
Was too close, with its breathing and thick hair
For him to judge. The floor was rotten; the sky
Was plastered halfway up with glass-smooth dung.
Light-lashed, self-righteous, above moving snouts,
The pigs' eyes followed him, a cheerful stare-
Even to the sow that always ate her young-
Till, sickening, he leaned to scratch her head
But sometimes morning after drinking bouts
(he hid the pints behind the two-by-fours),
The sunrise glazed the barnyard mud with red
The burning puddles seemed to reassure.
And then he thought he almost might endure
His exile yet another year or more.
But evenings the first star came to warm
The farmer whom he worked for came at dark
To shut the cow and horses in the barn
Beneath their overhanging clouds to hay
With pitchforks, faint work lightning, catching light,
Safe and companionable as in the ark.
The pigs stuck out their little feet and snored.
The lantern- like the sun, going away
Laid on the mud a pacing aureole.
Carrying a bucket along a slimy board,

He felt the bats uncertain staggering flight,
His shuddering insights beyond his control
Touching him. But it took him a long time
Finally to make up his mind to go home.

15. i am poem

15. I am poem

I am a shining star

I wonder why some people have to be so mean

I hear people say mean thing to each other

I see the world as a magical place

I want others to see the world like I do

I am a shining star.

I pretend the world is a magical place

I feel we should take care of the world we live in.

I touch animals and wonder why anyone would ever hurt them

I worry one day the world could become a big garbage

Dump

I cry when I hear the people are killing other people

I am I shining star

I understand that I can make a difference in the world

I say others can too

I try to be a positive role model

I hope people become less selfish and help others

I am a shining star

16. the guest house

16. The guest house
This being human is a guest house
Every morning a new arrival
A joy, a depression, a meanness,
Some momentary awareness come
As an unexpected visitor
Welcome and entertain them all
Even if they're a crowd of sorrows
Who violently sweep your house
Empty of its furniture
Still, treat each guest honorably
He may be clearing you out
For some new delight
The dark thought, the shame, the malice,
Meet them at the door laughing,
And invite them in.
Be grateful of whoever comes
Because each has been sent
As a guide from beyond

17. another time

17.ANOTHER TIME
For us like any other fugitive,
Like the numberless flowers that cannot number
And all the beasts that need not remember,
It is to-day in which we live.
So many try to say Not Now,
So many have forgotten how
Top say I Am, and would be
Lost, if they could, in history
Bowing , for instance with such old-world grace
To a proper flag in a proper place
Muttering like ancients as they stump upstairs
Of mine and his or ours and Theirs.
Just as if time were what they used to will
When it was gifted with possession still,
Just as if they were wrong,
In no more wishing to belong.
No wonder then so many die or grief,
So many are so lonely as they die;
No one has yet believed or liked a lie:
Another time has other lives to live

18. poetry

18. POETRY

You are far away from poetry ,but you are still
Poetry
Your eyes like a language , which speaks lots of
Thought
Your face a drop of rain that unwontedly
Separates from a cloud
And makes the earth a great view.
Actually, your eyes are like an ocean where so
Many tornados
But still there in some corner a long silence.
I want to reach that silence. I want to hear your
Maze which is hidden behind your smile.
No doubt you're so beautiful but I want to
Explore that part which is hidden from all
I want to make a poem with help of your words,
Your eyes , and with your silence.
You still you ever and you forever make me
Uncomfortable and I'm enjoying that uneasiness.

19. don't give up

19. DON'T GIVE UP
Hey don't give up you are not something like a
Glass cup
That you will break so easily
Tears may be falling from your eyes like it's
Drizzly but
You still have in you left some strength
You are not broken you are just bent
I know the journey is long it makes you tired
And I also know that you are very strong
You have chosen unique goals
Such goals that when some thing of
Accomplishing them shiver their souls
You are like a bird
Whose wings have been injured
You must heal and once again fly in the sky
This time a bit more high the challenges are
Great but you don't need to be a afraid
Remember your goal is to become the voice of
The oppressed
Your goal is to help the depressed
Your dream is to make your father's dream Come true
Your dream is to right a poem that can only be written by a few

20. first love

{ every one has a first love in their life, it's a very fascinating story for stuti well she did had a first love at time of her 5th standard... crazy right.. her first love was insane. But the heartbreaking part was when she confessed her feeling the answer came was no... that time her best friend was left to console her... she decided to write a special book just based on her first love}

20. First Love

I ne'er was struck before that hour
With love so sudden and so sweet
His face it bloomed like a sweet
Flower
And stole my heart away complete
My face turned pale as deadly pale
My legs refuse to walk away
And when he looked what could I
All?
My life and all seemed turned to clay.
And then my blood rushed to my face
And took my eyesight quite away
The trees and bushes round the place
Seemed midnight at noonday,
I could not see a single thing,
Words from my eyes did start
They spoke as chords do from the string
And blood burnt round my heart

Are flowers the winter's choice?

Is love's bed always snow?

She seemed to hear my silent voice.

Not love's appeals to know

I never saw so sweet a face

As that I stood before

My heart has left its dwelling place

And can hurt no more.

21. just he

21. Just HE
His eyes
His smile
His laugh
His style
His talks
his jokes
his breaths
his strokes
his hair
his curls
his warmth
his nerves
every bit of him
attracts me
with every bit of him
I fell in love

22. special one

22. special one
when you're with me there is nothing that can hurt
all the pain burning inside is just a dirt
I feel safe from inside
No matter what happens outside
You are my happiness I don't need anything
When I have you I have everything
Sometimes I listen one song over and over again
When my eyes create a flood out of tears rain
But when I see you all my happiness comes to me
All my problems flee flee just flee
I don't need anyone
When I have my special one
I am ready to live with you
Under the sky that is blue
I am waiting for that very beautiful day
When you will proudly say hey that's the one I love!
I am just 4.7 in height not short rather its cute
Because I can receive the best hug from my dude.
You have always been able to see the pain behind the fake smile
Even there is a light in darkness when you hold hand that is mine….!!

www.ingramcontent.com/pod-product-compliance
Lightning Source LLC
Chambersburg PA
CBHW031005180726
47993CB00018B/1577